10 CONVERSATIONS TO HAVE WITH YOUR PARTNER BEFORE YOU TAKE THE NEXT STEP

by Derrick Sobers

Inspired Forever Books
Dallas, Texas

Ten Conversations To Have With Your Partner Before You Take The Next Step

Inspired Forever Books

Dallas, Texas

(888) 403-2727

https://inspiredforeverbooks.com

Words with Lasting Impact™

Paperback ISBN: 978-1-948903-74-5

Printed in the United States of America

Disclaimer: This book is not any kind of religious documentation or text of any context. It is simply one person's perspective of the lessons learned, inspired by the reading of the Chapter of Proverbs (NIV edition). It is meant to be a source of learning for all people. Period.

TABLE OF CONTENTS

WHAT IS THE PURPOSE OF THIS BOOK?

For most of us, love has failed us many times. In hindsight, I realized I could have saved a lot of time and energy spent on the wrong person if I had just asked the right questions from the beginning. That's what this book is. The right questions. The right questions to determine if your partner has the same values and morals upon which you can build a successful foundation.

Warning: these questions will get very in-depth and challenging. Because some conversations are tough but necessary.

HOW TO READ THIS BOOK

One question at a time. These questions are meant to generate your own questions you may have for your partner, but I recommend reading these with anyone with whom you wish to grow closer: parents, best friends, children.

So if a question from this book makes you think of twenty more questions of your own . . . even better. This book's only intent is to provide you and your partner with a crash course in getting to know each other. The more conversations you have, the more you understand who the other person is. Make sure not to interrupt each other, but let the conversation go where it goes. It is important to know that a lot of these questions are open ended so the person answering can give their own interpretation of a response. A few things to remember:

- Be ready to be transparent with one another.
- There are no right or wrong answers.
- Focus not only on the responses but also on the way they answer (body language, tone, connotation, articulation, confidence).
- Don't interrupt when someone is responding.
- Answer each question entirely before moving on to the next one.

PRIMARY
CONVERSATIONS

LOVE

What is love to you? (Use only three words.)

How would you know that your partner loves you?

How do you show your partner you love them?

Who is the one person you've loved the most?

How do you know if someone deserves all your love?

What scares you about giving all your love to someone?

Talk about a time when you wanted to give someone your love, but they proved they didn't deserve it.

Describe your love in three adjectives.

What are some bad habits you do toward someone you love?

What have you learned that you shouldn't do when you're in love?

What have you learned that you should do more of when you're in love?

What is the most important lesson you have learned about yourself when you're in love?

Were you raised on survival or love?

How did your parents give you love?

Do you consider yourself a lover or a fighter?

When was the last time you had to fight for love?

What keeps a relationship together besides love?

What material thing do you love right now? Why?

How effective are you at showing someone you love them? (On a scale of 1–5.)

What is the best part about being in love?

What is your biggest obstacle to finding love right now?

COMFORT

What is a comfortable life to you? (Use three words.)

When you are in the most comfortable version of your life, answer the following questions:

- How much money will you make? (Minimum salary to be comfortable.)
- How many friends will you have?
- What is your relationship status? (single or married)
- How many children?
- What industry will you work in?
- Where would you live?
- What will your hobbies be?

How comfortable are you with your life right now? (Scale of 1–5)

What will increase your comfort level right now?

What will decrease your comfort level the most right now?

What is the most uncomfortable you have ever been?

Are you more comfortable staying at home or going out on the weekends?

What social setting makes you uncomfortable?

What social setting used to be enjoyable but now makes you uncomfortable?

Right now, would you rather be single or in a relationship? Why?

How comfortable are you with change? (Scale of 1–5)

Rate how comfortable you are in the following scenarios on a scale of 1–5:

- Making healthy lifestyle changes
- Making changes to your diet
- Making a career change
- Changing a work process at your current job

- Changing to act more friendly
- Spending less money
- Making addiction changes (alcohol, drugs, food, smoking, etc.)
- Making changes that your partner wants you to make
- Making changes that your partner asks of you but that you disagree with
- Unlearning behaviors from past relationships
- Moving to a new state and being alone
- Quitting your job and raising the kids
- Being with a partner who already has kids
- Understanding without agreeing
- Being okay with your partner quitting their well-paying job (over $100k salary) to follow their dream job ($30k salary)
- Talking about sex
- Taking rejection
- Selling someone something
- Admitting you're wrong
- Taking physical pain
- Forgiving and forgetting
- Being around people who don't want you there
- Being at an event that you don't enjoy but your partner does
- Letting people borrow money
- Asking for money
- Asking for help

RELATIONSHIPS

Right now, how good of a partner are you? (1–5)

What qualities do you have that make you a good partner?

Are you "relationship ready" right now?

Describe your perfect relationship.

What obstacles prevented your last relationship from being successful?

What are your three worst qualities?

What is a way that you've sabotaged a relationship before?

What's a bad habit you've had to unlearn from past relationships?

Are you actively looking for a relationship right now? How?

Are you on any dating sites?

Have you been on any dating sites?

How have you been scarred from past relationships?

What issues prevent you from becoming a better partner?

What do you think your perfect partner will be like? Consider the following:

- How tall will they be?
- How much will they weigh?
- What body type will they have?
- What kind of job will they have?
- What kind of family will they come from?
- How much will they work out?
- What kind of education will they have?
- Will their family be upper, middle, or lower class?
- What will be their three best qualities?

What are your three best qualities?

How do you expect your partner to balance you?

What will attract you to your partner besides looks?

Are you comfortable dating someone rich?

Are you comfortable dating someone poor?

Would you rather date someone rich or poor?

What will fifty/fifty effort be in your household?

Who will do the cooking?

Who will do the cleaning?

Who will run around with the kids?

Who will buy groceries?

Who will handle repairs around the house?

Who's responsible for the majority of the bills?

What will be your favorite chore of the house?

How should your partner handle you being upset? (Distance or Communication)

What are your love languages right now?

What are some signs that your relationship is ending?

What are your three red flags?

What are your three green flags?

Who comes first, your parents or your partner?

What good things did you learn from your parents about relationships?

What bad things did you learn from your parents about relationships?

MONEY

What's your salary?

Show each other your bank accounts.

What do you spend the most money on? (In each category: bills, expenses, recreational.)

How much debt do you have? (College loans, credit cards, and loans.)

What's your credit score? (Pull it up and show each other.)

How financially literate are you? (Scale of 1–5)

Who taught you financial literacy?

How aggressive are you at paying off your debts? (Scale of 1–5)

Name three scenarios that would be worth going into debt by $50k? $100k? One million? (Medical? Opportunity? Leisure?)

What is the dumbest thing you have gone into debt for?

Among your friend group, who is the most motivated to get rich? What do they do in following that goal?

What are three short-term goals you can pursue in order to be wealthy long term?

Where do you get your education about money?

Have you ever been poor?

How would you handle waking up tomorrow with no money?

What warning would you give the teenage version of yourself involving money?

What are the three best investments you could make right now?

How did your parents invest in your future?

What is the way you are going to invest in your future?

What is the best book you have ever read about money?

What is something you spend money on that you wish you could stop buying?

What is your guilty pleasure?

What is a healthy amount to spend on a vacation? (Domestic and international.)

Do you agree that the love of money is the root of all evil?

How has focusing on only the money caused you to make mistakes?

When is it a good idea to take a job with a lower salary than your current job?

Would you take a job you hate for $100k? For how long?

If your partner was awarded one million dollars, how would that change your lifestyle?

Are you generally good or bad with money?

If someone gave you one thousand dollars, what would you do with it? (What if it was $10k? $100k?)

GOALS

What's your biggest goal in life?

What goal are you most proud of? (Besides family.)

What's your next goal?

Who is the biggest supporter of your goals?

Are you self-motivated?

What is your biggest asset?

What quality will be your biggest tool on the road to success?

What is your ultimate goal in life?

What goals did you previously want but no longer want? Why?

HEALTH

What medical conditions do you have? Mental illness? Physical? Emotional?

What conditions run in your family?

What do you do to prevent the medical conditions in your family from happening to you?

What conditions or behaviors did your parents have during your childhood?

What medical condition are you most scared of getting?

What medical condition or injury are you scared of your partner getting?

What kind of medical condition could your partner have that would be grounds for leaving them? (STDs, addictions, etc.)

How long would your partner have to be brain dead for you to "pull the plug" if they were in the hospital?

If you had to choose between your partner or your newborn baby, which would you choose?

EDUCATION

What's the highest level of education you've completed?

What's the highest level you wish you could have completed?

What has stopped you from achieving your educational goals?

What education do you think is the best for you? (College, trade school, other.)

What kind of learner are you? (Auditory, visual, hands on, repetition, other.)

What is the educational level of your parents?

What kind of education did your parents encourage for you?

Did you do what your parents wanted you to do?

What has been your favorite part about your education so far?

What was your favorite subject in high school?

Besides the credentials, what value does your education provide you?

How will your education prepare you for success?

Do you believe education is worth going into debt? Why or why not?

Do you already have college debt? How much?

RELIGION

What religion were you raised in?

Did your family practice their religion growing up?

Could you date someone who practiced a different religion?

Is your partner's spirituality a big deal to you?

Would you be okay with your partner not taking interest in your religion?

Why did you choose to practice the religion that you participate in?

Are you trying to grow in your religion? Why?

How does your religion impact your life?

What would happen to you if you didn't have your religion as a support system?

SEX

Should a person know how to sexually satisfy their partner from the beginning, or does it happen over time?

When is it appropriate to discuss sexual preferences?

Are you comfortable telling your partner you do or don't like something during sex?

Do you feel it is important to talk about sex on the first date?

What makes a bad sexual partner?

What makes a good sexual partner?

Do you believe you can build sexual chemistry with a partner you're not attracted to initially?

Would you consider sexual education? Would you rather be by yourself or with your partner?

Would you consider yourself sexual? (Scale of 1-5)

What does it take for you to get comfortable enough to consider a partner sexually?

What could your partner do that would "turn you off" sexually?

What are some nonsexual qualities that turn you on?

On average, how long does it take for you to get sexually comfortable with your partner?

EMOTIONAL INTELLIGENCE

In your own words, what's emotional intelligence?

Give an example of how you reacted the wrong way because of a lack of emotional intelligence.

Give an example of how emotionally intelligent vs. non-emotionally intelligent people behave differently in the following relationships:

- With their partners
- With their children
- With their parents
- In social settings
- With coworkers

How does someone with emotional intelligence act differently, generally?

How did you learn emotional intelligence?

How would you teach emotional intelligence to your children?

How did your parents teach you emotional intelligence?

What have you gained since you learned emotional intelligence?

What have you lost before because you didn't have emotional intelligence?

What demographic of people do you think needs to learn emotional intelligence the most?

SUPPLEMENTAL CONVERSATIONS

SUCCESS

Right now, do you consider yourself successful?

Will you be successful in ten years? Twenty years?

What is preventing you from being successful right now?

What is your dream job? Why is that your dream job?

Would it still be your dream job if you had a zero salary?

What do you consider success? (Three words.)

What do you consider a successful partner?

What are you doing now to be successful later?

Do you agree with the statement "To be great, you have to give up something good"? What will you sacrifice to be great?

Do you want to be great?

What is your version of "being great"?

Put these four things in order according to priority:

- Making money
- Being morally good
- Being spiritual
- Taking care of family

Who is the most successful person you know?

What changes have you recently made to help you be more successful?

What do you need to unlearn right now?

What toxic behaviors have you fixed so far?

Which toxic behaviors are you working on right now?

Who is the person stopping you from being successful?

What is the biggest help you can receive right now to help you on the road to success? (Besides money.)

Does success mean making a lot of money?

What is your definition of success?

HEALING

Are you healed?

How are you healing?

Have you gone to a licensed therapist?

Do you think a licensed therapist is necessary?

What does someone on the path to healing look like?

What are some things people do differently when they are healed?

How would you help your friends heal?

How would you help your children heal?

How would you help your partner heal?

How did you figure out that you needed to heal?

What problems do you have because you weren't healed?

What will be your first step to healing?

How will you know you're done healing?

Are your parents healed?

PRIORITIES

What's your priority right now? Why is that your priority?

What was your priority five years ago?

Why did your priorities change?

What's your life's priority? (What will you want to have achieved at the end of your life?)

How could money affect your priorities?

How could family affect your priorities?

Once you become financially successful, how will your priorities change?

RETIREMENT

What are your plans for after you retire?

Would you still work after you retire?

Describe your first six months after retirement. Ten years.

How will your priorities change after your retirement?

Are you planning to retire from your current organization? If not, why are you still there?

What would be your perfect job to retire from? What's stopping you from getting that job?

Will you give your family more or less effort when you retire?

Will you consider yourself "done" when you retire?

What words will describe how you'll feel when you finally retire?

What is the next goal after retirement?

How will you help society after retirement?

CHILDHOOD

Did you grow up on love or survival?

What is your best childhood memory?

What is your worst childhood memory?

Where did you grow up? (City, suburbs, or rural.)

Did you grow up upper, middle, or lower class?

What did you want as a child but never got?

What did you get as a child but didn't want?

What was a major strength your parents had that helped your family?

What was the biggest way your father impacted you?

What was the biggest way your mother impacted you?

What was the most valuable lesson you learned growing up?

What's a lesson you had to unlearn as an adult?

Did your parents spank you?

PARTNERSHIP

What do you need from your partner besides love?

Would you be okay working with your partner?

If you started a business with your partner, what would you have them be in charge of? Why?

Would you prefer your partner:

- Be an introvert or an extrovert?

- Work a nine-to-five or be an entrepreneur?

- Be educated with debt or uneducated without debt?

- Be quiet or loud?

- Have a salary of $100k with $200k of debt or salary of $40k with no debt?

- Be very successful and always busy or have average success with a great work-life balance?

- Be fit with average IQ or have an average body with a high IQ?

- Be personable and average looking or socially awkward and very beautiful?

- Be worth $100k but never buys you nice things or worth $50k but spoils you?

- Be average looking but satisfies you sexually or beautiful but doesn't satisfy you?

- Be adventurous but living paycheck to paycheck or successful and boring?

- Have a salary of $150k a year with three kids (from past relationships) or a salary of $50k a year with no kids?

- Be traditional or modern?

- Be ten years older and successful or the same age but will be successful in ten years?

RAGE

How often do you get mad?

When was the last time you got angry?

When you are upset, do you need space or communication?

Do you turn physical when upset?

What's the easiest way to make you angry?

How have people accused you of upsetting them?

When was the last time you realized you were wrong?

How do you react in stressful situations?

When was the last time you broke down?

When is the lowest you have ever felt about yourself?

Talk about a time when you isolated yourself.

FRIENDS

Who's your best friend? Why are they your best friend?

Did you have a lot of friends in high school? How about now?

Do you prefer your friends to be introverted or extroverted?

Describe the best moment you've had with your friends.

How good of a friend are you? (Scale of 1–5)

What are your worst qualities as a friend?

What's a time you confronted a friend?

How much of an enabler are you? (Scale of 1–5)

Do you do well with feedback?

Talk about a time you changed your behavior because of feedback.

Talk about a time you had to cut off a friend.

Talk about a time when you've been a toxic friend.

Do you believe your friends should come before your partner?

When have your friends guided you to make a bad decision?

What are your friends ambitious about?

Which one of your friends is most likely to confront you?

How likely are you to confront friends? (Scale of 1–5)

How would your friends describe you? (Three words.)

EXPECTATIONS

As a wife or husband, what will you provide for your spouse?

What do you expect your partner to bring to the table?

What do you expect your partner's major priorities to be?

What are certain tasks that you will never do?

What are tasks you dislike but will do?

After a long day of work, when you come home what do you expect your partner to be doing?

After a long day of work, what will your priorities still be?

What kind of expectations did your parents have for each other?

What kind of expectations do you have for your best friends?

Do you expect your and your partner's careers to balance each other's, or will you both do your own thing?

Do you think expectations will change over time?

DRUGS

Do you use medicine regularly or as a last resort?

What kind of recreational drugs have you taken? What do you want to take?

If you could take a drug to instantly make you the happiest you can be, what would the drug do for you?

If a drug could take away any toxic behavior or quality you have, what would you want to have fixed about yourself?

If a drug could give you more of a positive quality or emotion, what would you hope it gave you?

What kind of environment would make you comfortable to try new recreational drugs?

Would you rather do drugs in public or private?

CHILDREN

Do you have children?

Do you want children?

What conditions would make you ready for children?

Why do/don't you already have kids?

What three words would describe the parent you will be?

What's your number one priority as a parent?

What lessons did you learn in your childhood that you are going to teach your children?

Rate each one of your parents on how good of a parent they were to you. (Scale of 1–5)

What obstacle do you think you will experience that will prevent you from being a good parent?

When you think of what your children will look like, what do you picture?

Do you believe in abortion under the right circumstances? What circumstances would warrant abortion?

If you found out you were expecting a child right now, how would you feel? What would you want to do?

What is the main way you would show your children you love them?

How would you provide for them?

What excites you about having children?

What will be your preferred work-life balance as a parent?

What is your ideal job as a parent?

What would you say was your parents' biggest mistake while raising you?

Could you raise a disabled child?

Would you choose to abort a disabled fetus?

www.ingramcontent.com/pod-product-compliance
Lightning Source LLC
Chambersburg PA
CBHW081159090426
42736CB00017B/3388